THE SACRAMENTS
AND
THE BIBLE

The Sacraments
and
the Bible

Measuring the Salvationist viewpoint

alongside Scripture

Philip Layton

First published in 2007 by
Shield Books
© The Salvation Army
UK Territory Literary Unit
101 Newington Causeway,
London SE1 6BN

ISBN: 978-0-85412-755-9

Scripture quotations are taken from the
HOLY BIBLE, NEW INTERNATIONAL VERSION.
Copyright © 1973,1978,1984 by International Bible Society.
Used by permission.

SHIELD
BOOKS
© The Salvation Army
United Kingdom Territory with
the Republic of Ireland

CAPTAIN PHILIP LAYTON has a dual appointment as The Salvation Army corps officer at Hythe in Kent, where he serves alongside his wife, Karen, and as Tutor in New Testament Studies at William Booth College, London.

Phil is a member of The Salvation Army's Moral and Social Issues Council in the United Kingdom and a corresponding member of its International Doctrine Council. His commitment to the wider church is exercised as Chairman of the Hythe and Saltwood District Churches Council of Churches Together.

Formerly a Computer Presentations Designer, Phil undertook a variety of challenging and creative tasks, but the majority of his time was spent on corporate web site production, breaking new ground during an era when many companies were uncertain as to the benefits of the internet.

He has vocational qualifications in Management and in Information Technology, while academic studies include a BA (Religious Studies) from the University of Kent and a Master of Theology from Heythrop College, University of London in which he focused on uses and abuses of the Bible, ethics, and the Gospels.

The Laytons have two children; Anastasia and Joshua, and to relax Phil simply enjoys being with his family, playing or watching football, mountain climbing, swimming, or dreaming of a getaway to the Canary Islands!

We believe that the Scriptures of

the Old and New Testaments were given

by inspiration of God;

and that they only constitute

the Divine rule of Christian faith and practice.

Thank you Jesus!

With deep gratitude and ineffable love to
Karen
Anastasia & Joshua

Contents

Foreword

by
General Shaw Clifton

G OD LED William and Catherine Booth, together with those of influence around them in the earliest days of Salvationism, through much heart-searching and theological reflection before they reached the conclusion that it seemed pleasing to the Holy Spirit and to them (Acts 15:28) that The Salvation Army would no longer practice the outward observance of formal sacramental ceremonies.

The history of this and the cogent factors under-girding what has often been regarded as a lonely doctrinal stance have been well documented by Salvationist writers and others. Every Christian church denomination recognises the need to restate and re-teach its doctrinal truths afresh to every generation of believers.

The Army is no exception.

For that reason I welcome most warmly this latest contribution to the literature on The Salvation Army and the sacraments and, on behalf of Salvationists everywhere, record warm thanks to Captain Philip Layton for his most helpful work. The Captain's hope has been to articulate the Army's position from a Scriptural viewpoint. He has done so admirably.

My prayer is that this book will be used of God to help a new generation of Salvationists understand and, when called upon to do so, explain the Army's position; that it will also speak to those in the sacramental traditions, where we find many who, while not adopting our practice, nevertheless understand and affirm us in our teaching; and that Salvationists everywhere will capture anew that gloriously Christ-honouring vision of becoming living proof that, by divine grace, a holy life can be lived without reliance upon outward sacramental ceremony.

This is the God-given calling of every Salvationist.

International Headquarters
Queen Victoria Street
London

CHAPTER 1

The big question

THIS BOOK has been produced as the result of several factors surrounding the perpetual debate regarding the observance of the Eucharist and baptism. It has been written with particular regard to how The Salvation Army can justify non-adherence to these ceremonies when the vast majority of Christian denominations hold these sacraments as being an intrinsic part of the Christian faith.

However, in the chapters headed 'We believe in baptism!' and 'Should we be observing the Eucharist?', I have deliberately tried to put forward a biblical rationale that is as free as possible from any particular tradition, upbringing, prior knowledge or reference to other publications on the sacraments which may lead to bias.

While I feel privileged to be a member of The Salvation Army, and immensely grateful for the upbringing and nurture I have received, being a Salvationist has only increased my desire to question 'Army' beliefs and practices. Early influences during my upbringing together with later academic studies have also served to encourage my attention to Scripture and determination not to be afraid of putting theories to the test. The views expressed within this book are purely based on personal study of the Bible, against which I believe any Salvationist viewpoint must be measured.

The factors which have driven this study are ones which I could not ignore any longer, as they have had a continued impact upon my ministry, my congregation, my community, and upon other individuals and congregations in this country and across the world.

These factors include:

- A belief that the sacraments of the Eucharist and baptism are an integral part of the Christian faith, and that without them any church ceases to be fully functional.

- Being challenged as to my own Christian 'credentials' by fellow ministers of local churches as a direct result of the stance of The Salvation Army upon this issue.

- An awareness that too few Salvationists have been taught any clear biblical rationale behind the stance their denomination takes.

- Having witnessed the testimony of good and sincere people who have proclaimed the necessity of the sacraments in order to ensure one has truly received salvation.

- And finally, open and honest discussions with certain friends and ministers who have even believed that such ceremonies can help in the salvation of those who have already died.

However, although the above factors in themselves are good enough reasons to produce this book, my primary aim is to respond to just one common factor, which can be summed up in the question:

> 'As the Bible clearly teaches that we are to observe the ceremonies of the Eucharist and baptism, is it not true that you (as a representative of The Salvation Army) are being both disobedient to our Lord Jesus Christ as well as demonstrating little regard for the authority of the Bible?'

My answer to this question will inevitably raise others regarding the consistency of doctrine and theology within The Salvation Army, along with the Army's understanding of those biblical texts which are associated with the sacraments.

Indeed, The Salvation Army's very first doctrine of faith emphasises the place and authority of Scripture within that denomination, and if this doctrine is being neglected, ignored, or glossed over with regard to the sacraments then it would surely call into question the authority of the Bible in other areas of faith and practice. Worse than this, though, would be to discover that allegations of disobedience to Christ Jesus were found to be true.

This question – whether one is being disobedient to Scripture – challenges the fundamental beliefs and ecclesiology of The Salvation Army, and indeed of any person, church, or society daring to take a similar stance toward the sacraments.

I have been asked this question on many occasions in various ways and degrees of intensity, as have many other Salvationists. On such occasions I would have liked time to give the answer in the detail which it deserves.

My hope is that fellow Christians who have asked or have been asked this question will find what follows to be useful, satisfactory, yet short enough to remain readable and accessible.

Throughout the book biblical quotations are taken from the New International Version (NIV).

Addtionally, it is always helpful to read the full context.

CHAPTER 2

A divisive issue

*Now the Bereans ... received the message with great eagerness
and examined the Scriptures every day
to see if what Paul said was true*

Acts 17:11

'AS THE BIBLE clearly teaches that we are to observe the ceremonies of the Eucharist and baptism, is it not true that you (as a representative of The Salvation Army) are being both disobedient to our Lord Jesus Christ as well as demonstrating little regard for the authority of the Bible?'

Before looking at what the Bible has to say, it is worth taking a brief glimpse at just how divisive the issue of observing the sacraments really is.

Clearly the above question discloses a basic division of beliefs within the Church, but it would be too shallow to think such divisions over the sacraments stop there. There are also divisions with regard to the following:

• **How many sacraments are there?**

Though most Protestant churches observe the two which we shall consider, the Roman Catholic Church observes an additional five.

- **How are they to be observed?**

  Even within Protestant denominations there is division with regard to how one is baptised. Some insist on immersion, as per its literal meaning, while others claim that merely sprinkling the water has the same effect.

- **At what age should one be baptised?**

  Some denominations believe that the person being baptised needs to understand what they are doing, and to have professed a faith in Christ Jesus, while other denominations are happy to baptise infants.

- **Who should baptise whom?**

  Some insist baptism can be performed only by an ordained minister. Others do not.

- **What actually happens when the Eucharist is observed?**

  Beliefs are divided, particularly between Protestant and Roman Catholic, over the doctrine of transubstantiation and whether or not the bread and wine actually turn into the body and blood of Jesus.

- **What sort of wine and bread can be used?**

  Even among Protestant denominations differences occur with regard to whether the wine can be substituted by grape juice, or any other drink for that matter. Even the type of bread used has caused divisions, with some imitating the original Supper by using unleavened bread.

- **Who is 'allowed' to administer this sacrament of Communion?**

  This question, too, continues to cause division, with regard to who may bless and distribute it. Some say it must be an ordained minister, others practise more freely the priesthood of all believers. You can imagine the further divisions still which are involved once the subject of female ministry (or Priesthood) is introduced!

These divisions merely represent many, many more which occur the further one delves into the detail behind each denomination's administration and doctrine of the sacraments.

Such divisions are by no means good enough reasons not to practise such ceremonies, but I mention these to highlight the fact that The Salvation Army's stance is by no means the only, nor necessarily the most controversial, cause of divisiveness surrounding beliefs about the place and practice of the sacraments.

In considering how divisive the issue of the sacraments can be, it may even be true to say that The Salvation Army's stance helps avoid a great deal more divisiveness than it causes, but again it must be recognised that such an argument is simply not good enough when it comes down to the question of obedience to Christ's words, and biblical authority.

In short, there is clearly a vast range of divisive problems connected with observing the sacraments, but the biblical problem of not observing them outweighs these.

CHAPTER 3

Time for self-assessment

THIS SHORT CHAPTER is probably the most important in terms of 'de-cluttering' before considering what follows. Essentially I am asking you, the reader, to carry out a degree of introspection with regard to what your current viewpoint is on the sacraments and why.

Unless we can individually ascertain through self-assessment where we 'stand' with regard to the 'why, where, and how?' of the Eucharist and baptism then we will not be able to go on to the next step of this process, which is to put all traditions, upbringing and even sacramental experiences and beliefs temporarily to one side. It is therefore vital to pause at this point in order to work through these crucial questions:

- **What do I believe to be true with regard to observing the sacraments?**

- **If I am asked whether I believe the Eucharist and baptism to be essential as an act of obedience, what would I reply?**

- **How would I back this up?**

- **Would I refer to the Bible? To my own experience? To our church's tradition? To my parents or upbringing?**

- **Have I ever assumed any doctrine to be true without questioning it?**

These questions may not produce the sort of answers we would want to share with anybody else, but to get the most out of this book it is essential to first be aware of what we believe and why, and to be willing to have these beliefs challenged. It may even prove beneficial to make a note of the answers.

Having done this, we have the most difficult task of needing to try and place all prior nurture, spiritual cultivation and possible presumptions to one side.

The next two chapters are not going to refer to any traditions, schools of thought, or personal experiences, so any teaching, customs, culture and practices which may influence one's perspective on the sacraments need to be 'forgotten' for a while.

This is not because they are necessarily invalid, but it is more of a precaution to enable us to consider the biblical texts as objectively as possible.

Far better at this point to ensure that these words of Jesus do not relate to us:

'You have let go of the commands of God and are holding on to the traditions of men.'

(Mark 7:8)

Any such 'traditions' and 'practices' can always be measured against the conclusions later, after having focused on what the Bible actually says.

For those who stand with Salvationists on the issue of the sacraments, this means that all the helpful words of both pragmatic and theological rationale from William and Catherine Booth, the Salvation Army's founding leaders and those they led, will temporarily have no significance. Neither will the Salvation Army history books, nor books which even tackle the sacraments from a Salvationist viewpoint.

Though these may, or may not, be valid in the wider discussion, for the time being we need to set them aside, to see how the Salvationist stance measures by using just the Bible.

Similarly, if the reader comes from a tradition which has always held these sacraments as an essential part of the Christian faith and the life of the Church, there will be the correspondingly difficult task of trying to imagine never having been to church before, never having observed these sacraments, and never having known about them at all.

In both cases this is a very difficult thing to do, and may take some time, but unless a serious attempt is made to approach this subject purely from a biblical perspective then the outcome will always be prone to a prior bias.

It may be worth revisiting this chapter on 'de-cluttering' at various stages within the book when appropriate.

CHAPTER 4

We believe in baptism!

CHRISTIANS HAVE little choice but to believe in baptism if they are to maintain that the Bible is their primary source of spiritual authority. Indeed, some would go further and say that the Bible is not just the primary authority on matters of faith, but also on matters of practice, and certainly of doctrine and ecclesiology. On which Scripture texts, then, do I base the statement, 'We believe in baptism'?

If most church-attendees, or indeed most ministers, were asked to point to a Scripture text that states the necessity of being baptised, I suspect that the vast majority of responses would quote from *Matthew 28:19*:

> *'Therefore go and make disciples of all nations, baptising them in the name of the Father and of the Son and of the Holy Spirit.'*

However, in studying this verse closely I cannot help noticing that Jesus here is not recorded by Matthew as saying 'be baptised', but 'do the baptising'. In other words, although it may well be in keeping with what Jesus meant, there does need to be a degree of caution when interpreting Jesus' words from this text.

If someone were to ask, 'Why should I be baptised?' then one could argue against using this verse on the basis that it actually says nothing about being baptised. Furthermore, it does explicitly say that Jesus told his eleven disciples to go out and baptise, yet how many Christians have actually followed that commandment personally by initiating someone into the faith through immersion (or otherwise)?

The quoted verse commands the disciple to be a baptiser, but it is often only assumed that it commands the disciple to be baptised. Ironically, then, there may be many good folk who have been water-baptised and use this text to question the validity of non-observance of this sacrament who, in the light of this same verse, may not be strictly obeying the commandment themselves!

Another favourite verse, but less frequently used, in favour of the necessity of water-baptism comes from *John 3:5*:

Jesus answered, 'I tell you the truth, no one can enter the kingdom of God unless he is born of water and the Spirit'.

However, the context is vital to our understanding. Where, in *John 3:1-7*, Jesus explains the concept of being 'born again', the enquirer does not understand this term, so asks how anyone could possibly be born for a second time, even going back into the womb!

It is in *this* context that Jesus says you must be born of water (naturally, through the womb), and of the Spirit (supernaturally, becoming a new creation in Christ). The very next verse, *John 3:6,* makes this clear;

'Flesh gives birth to flesh, but the Spirit gives birth to spirit.'

Therefore *John 3:5* is not to be understood as an instruction to be water-baptised and the question remains, on what do I base the title of this chapter? The answer is *Mark 16:16*, where Jesus said:

'Whoever believes and is baptised will be saved, but whoever does not believe will be condemned.'

It is worth noting at this point that both the *New International Version* and the *New Revised Standard Version* have footnotes informing the reader that not all ancient authorities include **Mark 16:9-20**.

The *NRSV* footnote explains: 'In most authorities verses 9-20 follow immediately after verse 8, though in some of these authorities the passage is marked as doubtful.'

The implications for **Mark 16:16** are double-edged. It could be regarded by some as having doubtful authenticity, although a late addition does not necessarily imply a false record of what Christ said. On the other hand, even if it is a late addition, it would demonstrate that it was the accepted viewpoint at a very early stage of Church development. Either way, the reasons to believe in its accuracy are persuasive.

It can be clearly seen here that, unless we adhere to a 'pick and mix' theology, the Bible confirms the simple statement 'We believe in baptism'. For these reasons, it is my opinion that this text from Mark would serve as a better premise for proposing the observance of baptism as a sacrament than either of the more commonly used texts from Matthew or John.

Even within these 'obvious', well-known and well-used Scripture passages we see how the Bible can be interpreted in many different ways, even misunderstood, and that we constantly need to review its interpretation in a fresh light.

The Bible indicates that it is valid to state 'We believe in baptism', and we must be able to say this if we are to agree with Jesus' recorded words, which I have no reason to doubt are accurate, and every reason to believe that the Gospel author would want to preserve.

The natural question which needs to be asked, though, is what this actually means.

What *is* baptism? We may know the word's derivation and how baptism was practised in the early Church, but what did that symbolise? What did it actually mean to be baptised – *according to the Bible?*

To start with, it would be equally dangerous to read the baptism texts with the presumption that they necessitate water (both then and now) as it is to presume that they do not. Indeed, if we place too heavy an emphasis on immersion in water as being necessary, rather than a preferred method, that could take us into very dangerous territory with regard to **Mark 16:16,** for then it could read: 'Whoever believes and is *immersed in water* will be saved…'

It is true that some people do believe water is an essential ingredient in the salvation process, but this is not consistent with the whole theme of the New Testament, that salvation is by grace through faith alone, and not by faith plus works/ritual/ ceremony. For example, Paul writes:

> *It is by grace you have been saved, through faith – and this not from yourselves, it is the gift of God – not by works, so that no one can boast.*
>
> **(Ephesians 2:8, 9)**

If, on the other hand, we are to remain open to biblical persuasion as to what baptism actually is, and consider that immersion in water may be just *one* method of being baptised, then the imperative link between water and salvation is relieved.

So what is biblical baptism?

There are numerous instances in Judaism where baptism used to be performed through water, eg when initiating converts to the faith, so it would have been a natural way of initiating new Christians into the Church too. The baptism of John the Baptist has its function defined for us in **Mark 1:4**:

> *And so John came, baptising in the desert region and preaching a baptism of repentance for the forgiveness of sins.*

We also read that Jesus himself was baptised:

Then Jesus came from Galilee to the Jordan to be baptised by John. But John tried to deter him, saying, 'I need to be baptised by you, and do you come to me?' Jesus replied, 'Let it be so now; it is proper for us to do this to fulfil all righteousness'.

(Matthew 3:13-15)

John was preaching a baptism of repentance, but surely Jesus was not seeking forgiveness for his sins, as he was without sin:

Therefore, since we have a great high priest who has gone through the heavens, Jesus the Son of God, let us hold firmly to the faith we profess. For we do not have a high priest who is unable to sympathize with our weaknesses, but we have one who has been tempted in every way, just as we are – yet was without sin.

(Hebrews 4:14, 15)

… so why, then, was he baptised?

The quotation above from Matthew's gospel says it was 'to fulfil all righteousness'.

In what sense did this baptism fulfil all righteousness? Possibly Jesus wanted to associate himself with John's message; maybe it was because John was of a priestly line descended from Aaron *(Luke 1:5)* and Jesus was being consecrated for divine service.

Either way, it was not odd because it was a part of Jewish life and – this is *very* important – Jesus was a Jew. It makes little sense, then, to decide to undergo baptism by immersion on the basis that it follows the example set by Jesus.

It is vital that we always remember Jesus was a Jew, as well as the fact that he had higher and deeper motives behind his actions which were not necessarily carried out in order to be copied in a parrot-like or ritualistic fashion.

Jesus was circumcised – and yet so much of Paul's message within his letters in the New Testament addresses the false teaching that all Christians should likewise be circumcised.

Though they may exist, I do not know of any Christians today who, on placing their faith in Christ, decide to be literally circumcised like him. Such action might seem misguided – but the same holds true when considering Jesus' water-baptism. What is more, Jesus was ultimately crucified but I doubt whether that is literally what God intends for all of us.

Jewish circumcision was literal, but it symbolised and foreshadowed the circumcision of our hearts **(Deuteronomy 30:6; Jeremiah 4:4)** interpreted by Paul thus:

> *For it is we who are the circumcision, we who worship by the Spirit of God, who glory in Christ Jesus, and who put no confidence in the flesh – though I myself have reasons for such confidence.*
>
> **(Philippians 3:3, 4)**

Similarly, Jewish sacrifices literally took place, but symbolised and foreshadowed what has now been carried out once and for all by Jesus Christ's sacrifice (It would be useful at this point to read **Hebrews chapters 9-10**, and **Acts chapter 15).** Thus it would be wise to consider the possibility that the ritual of a literal water baptism is not obligatory either but, like sacrifices and circumcision, it symbolises a spiritual reality.

This is just one piece of the sacramental 'jigsaw puzzle' presented within these pages. It may not all fit together yet, but there are many more pieces to make the picture complete. The next piece can be found in the words of John the Baptist as recorded in **Matthew 3:11** and **Luke 3:16**:

> *I baptise you with water for repentance. But after me will come one who is more powerful than I, whose sandals I am not fit to carry. He will baptise you with the Holy Spirit and with fire. John*

answered them all, 'I baptise you with water. But one more powerful than I will come, the thongs of whose sandals I am not worthy to untie. He will baptise you with the Holy Spirit and with fire.'

John the Baptist states clearly that although he baptised with water, Jesus would baptise with the Holy Spirit and fire! ... and yet ... where is there an instance of Jesus baptising at all? Surely this is an incredibly important absence! In fact, in a deliberate statement on the issue, John's Gospel emphasises that Jesus himself did *not* baptise

. . . in fact it was not Jesus who baptised, but his disciples.

(John 4:2)

The timing of the author's comment is crucial, merely adding the emphasis that although Jesus' disciples may have been baptising with water, Jesus himself did not baptise. It comes directly after he records that John the Baptist's followers had claimed that Jesus was baptising **(John 3:26)**, probably with water, but without specifying whether they were accurate in identifying Jesus when it may have been his disciples they saw.

So it seems the Gospel author was just accurately recording what they had reported back to John the Baptist. Similarly just a few verses beforehand **(John 3:22)** we cannot be sure that Jesus himself actually baptised anyone. It could be similar to the story of Sir Christopher Wren, famed for building St Paul's Cathedral in London, yet he never laid a stone!

Following these claims the author inserts this helpful detail of extreme importance and, as if to anticipate such questions in our time, most effectively and deliberately clears the matter up for his readers just a few verses on:

The Pharisees heard that Jesus was gaining and baptising more disciples than John, although in fact it was not Jesus who baptised, but his disciples.

(John 4:1, 2)

So here is a situation within the Gospels where John the Baptist said Jesus *would* baptise with the Holy Spirit and fire, yet it is equally clearly stated that Jesus did *not* physically baptise with water. Either these verses conflict with one another, or to be baptised by Jesus can be something very different from being under water.

This matches John the Baptist's own message;

'I baptise you with water. But . . .'

(Luke 3:16)

Further, to describe the baptism of Jesus as being 'with *fire*' is the very opposite terminology to that which had occurred in *water*. Surely the contrast between the elements mentioned is deliberate, signifying that the baptism Jesus offered was on a higher or more intimate spiritual level.

Perhaps, some may say, this shift is similar to that which occurred from a literal to a spiritual circumcision, or from literal sacrifices to a spiritual faith in the ultimate sacrifice.

What more can be learnt about the act of baptism according to the Bible? We read of Paul asking some disciples:

'Then what baptism did you receive?' 'John's baptism', they replied. Paul said, 'John's baptism was a baptism of repentance. He told the people to believe in the one coming after him, that is, in Jesus.' On hearing this, they were baptised into the name of the Lord Jesus.

(Acts 19:3-5)

Firstly, we can see that although water may have been used, whether sprinkling, immersion, or otherwise, this is simply an assumption, for there is no mention of water, and indeed 'On hearing this they were baptised' could almost suggest that the baptism was automatic and spiritual. In this case such a suggestion is improbable, but care needs to be taken nonetheless of any presumptions.

Secondly, and more importantly, it is evident that this second baptism was needed. The first was a baptism of repentance. The second was a baptism into the name of Jesus. It is almost as if baptism is a statement of belief, whether it be one of a belief in needing forgiveness, or a belief in who Jesus is. This realisation is crucial, so allow me to restate it:

The fact that a second baptism was needed, from a baptism of repentance to a baptism into the name of Jesus, strongly suggests the meaning of baptism – that it was a statement of belief.

If this definition of baptism is used, then, to aid a comprehension of the great commission from *Matthew 28:19*, we can understand it as follows:

from –

Therefore go and make disciples of all nations, **baptising them in the name of** *the Father and of the Son and of the Holy Spirit,*

to –

Therefore go and make disciples of all nations, **so that they affirm the belief in** *the Father, the Son, and the Holy Spirit.*

We can see that theologically this makes sense too, claiming it is one's faith that matters with regard to salvation, and not the water or ceremonial traditions in themselves.

Paul provides further biblical evidence to substantiate this:

For I do not want you to be ignorant of the fact, brothers, that our forefathers were all under the cloud and that they all passed through the sea. They were all baptised into Moses in the cloud and in the sea.

(1 Corinthians 10:1, 2)

Now it is evident that Paul, a devout Jew, is speaking to a Jewish audience as it would have been *Jewish* ancestors who followed Moses.

But how can anyone be baptised 'into Moses'?

The answer is, 'in the same way as one is baptised into the name of the Father, Son, and Holy Spirit'. In other words it is a confession of who one follows, believes in or claims allegiance to.

As all of us are preconditioned in some way, socially, culturally, and indeed theologically depending upon our individual circumstance and upbringing, these conclusions may be very difficult for some to accept, especially if we have been brought up to believe water immersion, or sprinkling, is essential, but I hope that the 'jigsaw pieces' are beginning to fall into place and that the logic of this thesis is emerging.

So far I have argued that the proposal 'we must be physically immersed in water because Jesus was' is not valid because we do not literally imitate other things he did, such as being circumcised, attending Jerusalem's Feasts, or observing the Passover. Jesus was doing what Jews were required to do.

John saying Jesus would baptise, *not* with water but with the Holy Spirit, implies he *would* nonetheless baptise. Indeed John's Gospel also *states* Jesus did not baptise with water *(John 4:1,2)* so there is definitely a baptism *outside* of water-baptism.

Baptism, as shown in Paul's letter to the Corinthians, was a method of confessing who one follows. The people were baptised as followers of Moses not merely in the sea, which they did not come into contact with, but also in the cloud. Therefore contact with water itself – we can now say with all biblical authority – is not a requirement, as Paul makes clear thus:

In him you were also circumcised, in the putting off of the sinful nature, not with a circumcision done by the hands of men but with the circumcision done by Christ, having been buried with him in baptism and raised with him through your faith in the power of God, who raised him from the dead.

(Colossians 2:11, 12)

Such practices which used to take place literally under the Jewish system are implemented spiritually under the new covenant. This suggests that obstacles to fellowship with God, whether they be priests, rules about cleanliness, specific rituals, or laws were removed to give us direct access to God himself.

Here is my assertion so far:

- **The Bible nowhere states that all Christians should be baptised by _water_ either for salvation or as a command.**

- **However, as the _Bible_ says we must be baptised – so we _must_ be baptised.**

- **The difference is that the baptism the New Testament speaks of is a spiritual baptism which occurs upon confession of who it is that we follow or belong to.**

- **In writing to the church at Ephesus Paul confirms this:**

There is one body and one Spirit – just as you were called to one hope when you were called – one Lord, one faith, one baptism; one God and Father of all, who is over all and through all and in all.

(Ephesians 4:4-6)

Paul in this context is trying to stress the importance of unity and to avoid divisiveness. Yet, given the varying types of baptism found within the Bible, with or without water, into John, Moses, and Jesus, and given also the many modern variations upon these themes, surely the 'one baptism' that Paul was speaking of is that which is superior, spiritual, and of the Holy Spirit – for if not this, then which of these others?

The Apostle Peter also confirms this thinking in his first letter, talking about the flood:

In it only a few people, eight in all, were saved through water, and this water symbolizes baptism that now saves you also – not the removal of dirt from the body but the pledge of a good conscience toward God. It saves you by the resurrection of Jesus Christ, who has gone into heaven and is at God's right hand – with angels, authorities and powers in submission to him.

(1 Peter 3:20b-22)

Again it can be seen that baptism is 'the pledge of a good conscience toward God', which can only truly happen through faith in Christ's atoning work, thus affirming the belief 'in the Father, the Son and the Holy Spirit.'

Jesus underwent the ultimate sacrifice, and it is belief in this that makes a person right with God – Christians are no longer bound by any specific ritual.

It was also Jesus who underwent the ultimate baptism by being buried and raised to life again – and so to confess a belief in this baptism (as the letter from Peter tells us) is what is required for salvation.

Now our baptism, affirmation of belief, or confession of allegiance *can* certainly be made through the symbolic act of a public demonstration in water. There is nothing wrong with that. It might even be the most effective way of helping people to profess their faith. But the water itself merely helps to symbolise the baptism which is a confession of belief and there will be many, many other ways in which the same affirmation of faith may be demonstrated, each equally valid in confessing our belief. This is in accord with the freedom from legalism and rituals which the Gospel brings to other areas of our lives too.

But further, I believe that the one baptism calls Christians to stand up and tell others who they follow no matter what circumstance they may be in, whether they have the opportunity to tell family, friends, work colleagues, or strangers at a bus stop or, as Paul did, fellow prison inmates.

This can be done without any physical symbolism and in the knowledge that the Triune God hears all such confessions of faith. Such freedom in the Spirit goes further still and is even more liberating when we consider how it enables baptism through affirming our belief corporately too. Confessing our belief whenever a testimony is shared with someone, or when that testimony or profession of faith is sung – either way, who can deny that our testimony is a confession of belief, and therefore a baptism too?

The amazing truth is that the more we dare to consider how the Bible defines the true meaning of baptism, the more freedom we discover in its implementation!

Such freedom, in fact, that one of the most famous baptisms in the whole of history is that of a criminal prisoner left hanging on a cross. Dying next to Christ Jesus, the criminal turned to the Lord, admitted his sin and acknowledged Jesus' innocence before pleading:

> *'Jesus, remember me when you come into your kingdom'.*
>
> *(Luke 23:42)*

What a last-minute conversion!

What a confession of faith!

What a baptism! – and without any water, affirming his belief in Jesus' true credentials and directly to Christ Jesus himself!

What freedom!

But was it valid? With no water and no ceremony, did it meet the criteria for salvation set by Jesus in *Mark 16:16?*

We only have to read Jesus' reply to the dying man to realise that baptism is truly a profession of faith, even if it is confessing belief directly to Christ himself!

Jesus answered him, 'I tell you the truth, today you will be with me in paradise'.

(Luke 23:43)

It is tempting to close this chapter right now, as surely this last piece of evidence is proof enough of the theory proposed within this chapter.

However, I have heard it said that the command to be baptised is meant to be in water, but water is only necessary if there is *opportunity* to use it. Therefore death-bed conversions, or that of the crucified criminal, are exceptional circumstances, exempt from the need for such a baptism.

I hope that the reader can clearly see that **Mark 16:16** shows no sign of any such exemption, and being such an important 'get-out clause' we would expect it to have been mentioned elsewhere within the Bible, but it is not.

The fact is that the crucified criminal next to Jesus received salvation that day, meeting the criteria of Mark 16:16, because he believed in Jesus Christ, and because he professed it to Christ himself.

The beauty of it all is that once we are free to think about baptism as described in the Bible in the way that a total stranger to Christian tradition might consider it, we can see that God, having provided release from the laws and rituals of the Old Covenant through the death and resurrection of Jesus Christ, would not require of his followers an obligation to be immersed or sprinkled with water in order to demonstrate their obedience!

It is to misunderstand all that Jesus did for us if we maintain the idea that the baptism spoken of *had* to be done with water.

This study has used Bible texts alone, deliberately trying to stay clear of any presumptions or traditions. As we have travelled full circle around the main baptism texts in the New Testament, there is just one more hurdle to overcome before concluding, and that is to revisit Jesus' words as recorded in the verse which inspired the title of this chapter:

'Whoever believes and is baptised will be saved, but whoever does not believe will be condemned.'

(Mark 16:16)

The only way that this study can remain consistent with this warning is to say that the verse can be interpreted as:

'Whoever believes and **confesses it** *will be saved, but whoever does not believe* (and hence automatically would not confess it) *will be condemned.'*

As we come toward the end of this chapter, can such an interpretation be validated by other Scripture? Compare, for instance, the above interpretation of **Mark 16:16** with a similar statement by Paul who, in **Romans 10:9, 10** wrote:

That if you **confess** *with your mouth, 'Jesus is Lord,' and believe in your heart that God raised him from the dead, you will be saved.*

For it is with your heart that you believe and are justified, and it is with your mouth that you **confess** *and are saved.*

The final confirmation of this study is seen in the agreement between these two statements.

Paul does not say that the 'confession' must be done in water, nor does he even call it baptism, and this is because his words and those of Jesus recorded by Mark are conveying exactly the same message.

To be baptised is to affirm belief in the Father, Son and Holy Spirit.

Conclusion

In putting all of these pieces together I believe that the final picture clearly proclaims that baptism is confessing your faith and what you believe.

The Bible says we must be baptised – yes – but that baptism is one of confessing who we believe in, who we follow, and although this may certainly be symbolised by water, the Bible has proven that it may also be done in many other ways, including directly to Christ himself.

The Bible testifies that Christ has provided this immense freedom. When we find ourselves in front of that heavenly judgement throne, God will not ask us how we were baptised, but simply whether we confessed his name.

Having reached these conclusions, then together we can say:

We believe in the authority of Scripture.

We believe in baptism!

CHAPTER 5

Should we be observing the Eucharist?

THE CEREMONY of the Eucharist is also known as the Lord's Supper or Communion or, usually in the Roman Catholic Church, as Mass. Is the Eucharist something that all Christians should be observing?

As with water baptism, the vast majority of churches would answer in the affirmative, despite the differences in administering the sacrament which have been noted in a previous chapter.

However, some churches and individuals are not convinced of the *necessity* of this sacrament, while others claim it is an essential part of the salvation 'process'. The question I would like to answer is: According to the Bible – is it necessary to observe the Eucharist?

If you have not done so already, now would be a good time to put this book down for a few minutes and ask:

- **What would I say if challenged on this issue, and could I back it up biblically?**

- **How have my own views been formed and cultivated? From where?**

- **Have I ever challenged my own views?**

- **Am I ready to 'forget' about traditions and assumptions and ask the Holy Spirit to guide me afresh on the subject from Scripture?**

Just as the proponents of water baptism, and possibly any other doctrine, may have a particular favourite text or passage to use from Scripture on which to base their stance, so the most common reference used by proponents for observing the Eucharist is *Luke 22:19-20*:

> *And he took bread, gave thanks and broke it, and gave it to them, saying, 'This is my body given for you; do this in remembrance of me.' In the same way, after the supper he took the cup, saying, 'This cup is the new covenant in my blood, which is poured out for you.'*

Now there is a school of thought amongst some scholars which suggests that *Luke 22:19b-20* is an additional comment, not contained within the original manuscripts, and as such is of dubious credibility.

There is also a line of reasoning that highlights the amazing scarcity of references to the Eucharist throughout the rest of the New Testament, again suggesting that it was not such an important feature of the Christian life.

However, for the purposes of this study I would like to make it clear that in my opinion the small number of relevant texts does not prove anything. We might equally, for example, claim that their scarcity suggests that most churches were observing the Eucharist in the correct manner, and so it did not need to be addressed frequently.

As for the above comment in Luke being a late addition – maybe it was, and maybe it was not. Such conjecture changes, it seems, from generation to generation. But even if this line of thought is proved to be true, it would take a great deal of confidence for any follower of the resurrected Christ to 'put words into his mouth', and if we are willing to believe that our Scriptures contain claims of words from Jesus that he did not actually say, then at what point do we start and stop believing the rest of the Bible? Besides which, Paul repeats this command in *1 Corinthians 11:23-25*, and, as we shall go on to discover, there is a compelling reason why Jesus would have said these words, whether or not recorded, in any case!

Therefore, let us start with the premise that our main text is accurate and correct. It is the most widely used biblical evidence for stating that Jesus inaugurated the sacrament of the Eucharist. However, there is another possibility – which I now consider a probability – as to what exactly Jesus was saying and doing in and through these words.

> *And he took bread, gave thanks and broke it, and gave it to them, saying, 'This is my body given for you; do this in remembrance of me'.*

(Luke 22:19)

The only requirement to proceed effectively is for us to try and put aside for a moment all church practice, opinions, and assumptions which we may have of what the Bible might say, and consider the standard of Scripture *alone*.

Imagine that you have come across this text, and the whole idea of observing the Eucharist, for the very first time! You will immediately become aware that Luke is the only Evangelist who records Jesus saying 'Do this in remembrance of me'. The others mention the meal of course, but do not include Christ's explicit command to continue doing it. But having said that, I believe that such a fact should never be decisive, for if Christ, through the Bible, is commanding us to do something, then there should be no need for the command to be repeated.

However, it is vitally important to remember that Jesus, and his disciples, were Jews.

We have seen the importance of this within the baptism chapter.

They were born as Jews and they lived Jewish lives.

Another important thing to note is that Jesus and his disciples did not merely decide to gather for a meal, but they were required to, under Jewish Law, for the Passover, and the Feast of Unleavened Bread.

When Jesus had finished saying all these things, he said to his disciples, 'As you know, the Passover is two days away – and the Son of Man will be handed over to be crucified.'

(Matthew 26:1, 2)

On the first day of the Feast of Unleavened Bread, the disciples came to Jesus and asked, 'Where do you want us to make preparations for you to eat the Passover?' He replied, 'Go into the city to a certain man and tell him, "The Teacher says: My appointed time is near. I am going to celebrate the Passover with my disciples at your house."' So the disciples did as Jesus had directed them and prepared the Passover. When evening came, Jesus was reclining at the table with the Twelve...

...While they were eating, Jesus took bread, gave thanks and broke it, and gave it to his disciples, saying, 'Take and eat; this is my body.' Then he took the cup, gave thanks and offered it to them, saying, 'Drink from it, all of you. This is my blood of the covenant, which is poured out for many for the forgiveness of sins. I tell you, I will not drink of this fruit of the vine from now on until that day when I drink it anew with you in my Father's kingdom.'

(Matthew 26:17-20, 26-29)

Think of the account of the original Passover in Egypt when God struck dead the firstborn in all homes without the mark of blood on the door, which led to the release of the Israelites into the wilderness and finally to reach the Promised Land.

According to Jewish Law, recorded in detail in **Exodus 12** and **Leviticus 23,** all Jews were to celebrate this event every year at the same time, beginning with the Passover on the 14th day of Nisan in the Jewish calendar, then, followed by the Feast of Unleavened Bread, it was to last eight days in all. This practice is still carried out by Jews today.

On the first day of the Feast of Unleavened Bread, when it was customary to sacrifice the Passover lamb, Jesus' disciples asked him, 'Where do you want us to go and make preparations for you to eat the Passover?' So he sent two of his disciples, telling them, 'Go into the city, and a man carrying a jar of water will meet you. Follow him. Say to the owner of the house he enters, "The Teacher asks: Where is my guest room, where I may eat the Passover with my disciples?" He will show you a large upper room, furnished and ready. Make preparations for us there.' The disciples left, went into the city and found things just as Jesus had told them. So they prepared the Passover.

(Mark 14:12-16)

Neither **Matthew 26:17, Mark 14:12,** nor **Luke 22:9** say anything about Jesus being asked by his disciples; 'where shall we go and prepare your last supper', but instead they record these words; 'where shall we go and prepare the *Passover* meal?'.

Jesus' mission was reaching a climax, and he was warning his disciples that he would soon die. Yet they were still all Jews, and the requirement of the eating of the Passover meal had to be met. Furthermore, even Jesus himself (*Luke 22:8*) sent Peter and John clearly with the intention of preparing the Passover meal.

So far then, by looking at the Scripture alone, we must come to the conclusion that, as Jesus and his disciples were all Jews, therefore they ate the Passover meal which on this occasion *became* the Last Supper also. (We need to confirm this in our own minds before continuing.)

As mentioned, Luke is the only Gospel writer to record Jesus saying 'Do this in remembrance of me' *(Luke 22:19)* so what are we to make of this command? Was it for us? Was it just for those in the room with him? Was it intended as a one-off? Was it to be repeated forever?

It is not a mystery. We merely need to put the pieces together, and open our minds to think outside of our own church traditions. For generation after generation the Passover meal had been celebrated by Jews at one specific time in remembrance of the 'great escape' from Egypt.

Now Jesus, who is *our* great escape and gate into the *ultimate* 'promised land', tells the Jews of the time not to carry out the meal in remembrance of that *former* glory, but of the *present* one. The focus is being switched from the past to the future, from prophetic history to an inaugurated eschatology, from remembering God's salvation through the Exodus, to remembering God's salvation through Christ himself.

Again it is vital to remember that Jesus, as a Jew, was required to 'fulfil all righteousness' hence his *Jewish* disciples were to do no less, but with a different angle now, a different perspective.

With the benefit of hindsight we can see how the feasts of Israel listed in **Leviticus 23** include not only the prophecy of Passover, but also Pentecost and others which are essentially prophetic in nature. Indeed the last three feasts recorded in **Leviticus 23** prophesy what is yet to come. Such a study belongs to a separate book, but the point remains that Jesus himself was highlighting to his Jewish followers that he *was* the fulfilment of such prophecy.

Therefore I believe Jesus was telling his *Jewish* followers not to carry out the festival in remembrance of the former redemption, but of the present one made through his self-sacrifice.

With this in mind we can re-read the same main text with a new emphasis. So often we place an emphasis on the 'doing', or 'remembering' words, but as they were Jews, and as they 'did' these things every year, at every Passover, we need to place the emphasis elsewhere. When we read the relevant command, the emphasis, instead, needs to be on Christ, and ought to go on the words 'my', and 'me':

> *And he took bread, gave thanks and broke it, and gave it to them, saying, 'This is **my** body given for you; do this in remembrance of **me**'.*
>
> ### *(Luke 22:19)*

This may be hard to digest, due to our preconceptions, but I hope that the size and nature of this book enables it to be read several times if need be, and that the logic and sense of it all may become clearer to the reader. I have not deviated from nor neglected Scripture. I have merely challenged the way that, over centuries, this command has been interpreted.

On many occasions the disciples and others met together to break bread. That should not automatically be confused with the Eucharist. It was more of a social gathering. But on one occasion Paul writes to the Corinthians with disgust about how they are observing this commandment, after which he adds:

> *For I received from the Lord what I also passed on to you: The Lord Jesus, on the night he was betrayed, took bread, and when he had given thanks, he broke it and said, 'This is my body, which is for you; do this in remembrance of me.' In the same way, after supper he took the cup, saying, 'This cup is the new covenant in my blood; do this, whenever you drink it, in remembrance of me.' For whenever you eat this bread and drink this cup, you proclaim the Lord's death until he comes.*
>
> ### *(1 Corinthians 11:23-26)*

As Paul adds this helpful comment to Luke's account, the first thing to note is that he says 'whenever you eat *this* bread' as opposed to just saying 'whenever you eat bread'. We can only assume that by specifying this bread he means unleavened bread, as per the Passover meal.

What about the question of when we should remember Christ in this way? Paul does not say whether it is weekly, daily, or monthly but 'whenever we drink this cup.' I think Paul knows that they will understand the command to Jews to fulfil the Passover meal by remembering Christ, and here he is emphasising that this is not some one-off, but something to be done at every Passover.

And have we ever considered why Jesus himself did not say how often to do this in remembrance of him?

For all we know, Jesus might have meant 'do this in remembrance of me just now only', or 'just once in a lifetime', or 'every day' or 'every Sunday in a communion service', but no! The truth is that he did not need to say how often to do it for one simple reason – it was to replace the Passover meal and thus was to occur once a year from 14th Nissan, as recorded in Jewish law. Therefore the disciples could celebrate Christ by fulfilling, not breaking their Jewish laws.

This line of reasoning also sheds further light on Jesus' words when he said:

'Do not think that I have come to abolish the Law or the Prophets; I have not come to abolish them but to fulfill them. I tell you the truth, until heaven and earth disappear, not the smallest letter, not the least stroke of a pen, will by any means disappear from the Law until everything is accomplished.'

(Matthew 5:17, 18)

Even after going through the vital 'de-cluttering' procedure outlined earlier in this book, this may be fairly difficult information to process, so allow me to restate the main points so far:

- The context of the main text is the Passover meal, where the Jewish Christ and his Jewish disciples gathered as per the Jewish custom to remember the deliverance of the Jews from the slavery of Egypt into the promised land.

- Christ tells his inner circle of disciples – who are Jews – to remember him, and to use the meal to remember his sacrifice, redeeming them from the slavery of sin, giving them access to the true promised land, which is heaven. All this was the prophetic purpose of having the meal in the first place.

- He does not say how often to do this, because they already know . . . only once a year, at each Passover, as per their Jewish custom.

So perhaps the next question is: 'Where did this leave the non-Jewish Christians?'

At the time of this meal mentioned in the Gospels there would have been very few, if any, Gentile disciples, especially in that room. Gentile Christians came later after the Jewish authorities rejected Christ leading the Christians to flee from Jerusalem and persecution, spreading the good news into Gentile territory as a result.

Christianity was not separate from Judaism at first. When eventually Gentiles were being converted at the same time as the Jews were rejecting Christ, only then did Christianity become a separate religion.

Even Paul, arguably Christianity's greatest ambassador, still held very strongly onto his Jewish upbringing through observing festivals and various traditions and laws.

Although his conversion taught him the necessity for the Messiah to suffer, and the futility of relying on the law for salvation, he nevertheless often confirmed that he was still a Jew.

Examples of this can be found in **Philippians 3:4-6** and
Romans 11:1. This is highly important and helpful to remember
as we think about the Christian practices of non-Jews, and look
at further Scripture.

> *When you come together, it is not the Lord's Supper you eat, for as*
> *you eat, each of you goes ahead without waiting for anybody else.*
> *One remains hungry, another gets drunk.*

> *(1 Corinthians 11:20-21)*

Paul condemns the Corinthians for their behaviour whilst
celebrating the Lord's Supper and then goes on to repeat the
command of Jesus Christ to them. But read the words of these
two verses carefully – the people were misusing the supper and
even getting drunk – in fact, he almost makes it sound like they
were having a feast! It is well worth noting here that Paul's
Corinthian audience were Jews;

> *For I do not want you to be ignorant of the fact, brothers, that our*
> *forefathers were all under the cloud and that they all passed through*
> *the sea. They were all baptised into Moses in the cloud and in the sea.*

> *(1 Corinthians 10:1, 2)*

So we have here the *Jewish* context in which Paul is writing.
It seems Paul knew that the Lord's Supper was more of a feast
or a meal rather than merely bread and wine. This would agree
with it being the Passover meal – tied in with the Feast of
Unleavened Bread, which is the bread that Christ broke when
he, too, spoke to a Jewish audience.

In another passage relevant to this argument, when Paul is
faced with charges that are *false* about him, his friends say:

> *'They have been informed that you teach all the Jews who live among*
> *the Gentiles to turn away from Moses, telling them not to circumcise*
> *their children or live according to our customs. What shall we do?*

They will certainly hear that you have come, so do what we tell you. There are four men with us who have made a vow. Take these men, join in their purification rites and pay their expenses, so that they can have their heads shaved. Then everybody will know there is no truth in these reports about you, but that you yourself are living in obedience to the law.'

(Acts 21:21-24)

About Paul, one of Christianity's greatest ambassadors, evangelists, and teachers, they said,

'*... everybody will know there is no truth in these reports about you, but that you yourself are living in obedience to the law'*!

Like Jesus and his disciples, Paul was a Jew, as he himself says:

'*I am a Jew, from Tarsus in Cilicia, a citizen of no ordinary city.'*

(Acts 21:39)

He did not stop being a Jew just because he had faith in Christ Jesus. His Jewish customs and practices were still to be observed because that was a part of being a Jew, and thus he taught all Jews to do the same, but along with the message of Jesus Christ.

The Lord's Supper, then, was not a new ceremony, but an old Jewish one which our Lord commanded Jews to carry out in remembrance of him.

Jesus spoke this command only to Jews, and similarly Paul's letter in which the Lord's Supper is mentioned is also addressed to Jews in Corinth. At no point do we read of Jesus, or Paul, commanding Gentiles to observe the Eucharist!

In other words – it was not a command for Gentiles!

Conclusion

So then, what would our answer now be if asked 'Should we be observing the Eucharist?'

Have we been able to put our preconceptions to one side?

Do we feel more comfortable with the view we now hold, and are we more confident of the place and authority of the Bible in relation to those beliefs?

Is there a significant text or group of texts which can sufficiently refute this chapter?

These are questions I have continually asked myself so, both convinced of my findings and satisfied that this study is grounded in Scripture alone, I now leave it with you to consider, pray about, and perhaps consider once more.

Obviously there is much in a communion service which is helpful. Such services can encourage us, they can help us concentrate on our Lord, and they can bring unity in parts of Christ's body. Communion might well be regarded as another word for fellowship, and thus communion may be practised in many varieties of Christian gatherings. One may say communion can be made at each meal time as we remember who it is that provides our every need, and that our remembrance of Christ's atoning work should be seen and lived out through our everyday lives.

But this study of Scripture has shown that for Gentile Christians, who are thus not bound by the Jewish customs and practices, the Eucharist is not obligatory. Jesus spoke the command of *Luke 22:19* in the company of Jews, in the setting of an annual Jewish custom, and similarly Paul's letter in which the Lord's Supper is mentioned is also addressed to a Jewish audience in Corinth. It was not a command for Gentiles!

It would take only one short step from saying such a ceremony is a command to all Christians, to saying that without participation in such a ceremony one is not a Christian. One can only imagine, and perhaps look forward to, the degree of disunity and divisiveness that might be avoided within the Church if only these Scripture texts were interpreted in the way outlined above.

Similarly, my hope is that those who do not observe the Eucharist (or water-baptism) may be much more confident and comfortable with communicating the Scriptural rationale for such non-observance. The Gospels did not record any falsehoods, nor has the Bible contradicted itself in this respect. Those who do not participate in the Eucharist are not being disobedient, and neither did Paul or the New Testament authors misrepresent Christ's command at that Passover meal.

The problem has been in too rigid an interpretation of Scripture, which has led to a misunderstanding of key texts, which in turn has led to traditional belief replacing Scriptural comprehension.

This is not a new problem, but has similarities to the discussions which led to the words of Jesus recorded in *Mark 7:8* and the Christian council's letter recorded in *Acts 15:22-29*.

That is why I hope this book has been helpful in some way to those who have been able to look at these biblical texts afresh.

Thank God for the Bible, our God-inspired guide to living and to the truth.

And thank God for Jesus Christ who died to take away all sin from whosoever places their trust in Him through faith alone, that we may spend eternity in the presence of the angels in heaven and come face to face with our Creator as Saviour.

And finally...

It is my prayer that this book may be an aid to spread the freedom its message implies and help liberate any Christian who has either felt obliged to observe the sacraments in their traditional form, or else in non-observance had feelings of inferiority or even guilt when faced with charges of dis-obedience to the Scripture passages from which the sacraments have been developed.

Keeping it short and hopefully 'easy to read' should enable and encourage the reader to retrace any of the steps I have made in order to be convinced of the content.

Throughout the work I have deliberately not used any source other than the Bible to reconsider the place of the sacraments. There are many good practical, historical, and other theological reasons for coming to the same conclusions, but in an attempt to stay well clear of traditions or cultures I have simply tried to put forward my case from a biblical perspective.

It seems to me that there has been a growing call for this, as no matter how valid or persuasive the rationale may be behind the non-sacramental arguments put forward in the past, more often than not the counter-argument involves a return to an understanding of what the Bible teaches.

However, there are some very helpful books which I would like to suggest for further reading, written from a Salvationist perspective, and which by taking into account practical, historical, theological, missiological and ecclesiological considerations tend to come to similar conclusions as we have within this biblical study.

Therefore, for those who would like to consider how solid the non-sacramental stance is from additional perspectives I sincerely recommend the following resources:

Look out for books online

A number of Salvation Army publications are now available online, among them two of the books detailed opposite — Philip Needham's *Community in Mission* and Clifford Kew's *Closer Communion.*

See www.salvationarmy.org.uk/library

Then click on books

The most comprehensive, academic study of The Salvation Army and its sacramental stance is to be found in *Sacraments and The Salvation Army* by R. David Rightmire, Scarecrow Press, 1990, ISBN 978-0810823969

Bibliographical Resources

Street, Robert, *Called to be God's People*,
The Salvation Army IHQ, London, 1999.

Clifton, Shaw, *Who are these Salvationists? An Analysis for the 21st Century*,
Crest Books, Alexandria, 1999.

The Sacraments; A Biblical-historical Perspective,
Issued by Authority of the Territorial Commander,
Canada & Bermuda Territory, 1992.

Needham, Philip, *Community in Mission; A Salvationist Ecclesiology*,
The Salvation Army IHQ, London, 1987.

Baptism, Eucharist and Ministry, WCC Commission on Faith and
Order, Paper no.111: *A Response from The Salvation Army*,
The Salvation Army IHQ, London, 1985.

Metcalf, William, *The Salvationist and the Sacraments*,
SP&S Ltd, London, 1965, Seventh edition 1981.

Kew, Clifford, *Closer Communion*,
SP&S Ltd, London, 1980.

Coutts, Frederick, *No Continuing City*,
Hodder and Stoughton, London, 1976.

Dean, Harry, *The Sacraments, the Salvationist Viewpoint*,
Issued by Authority of the General,
SP&S Ltd, London, 1960.

Carpenter, Minnie, *Salvationists and the Sacraments*
(A pamphlet reprinted from *William Booth, Founder of the
Salvation Army* by Minnie Carpenter, Epworth Press, 1942),
Campfield Press, St Albans, 1946 and 1954.